Posted Anonymously

Felix Flauta Jr.

First paperback edition November 2022

Cover Illustration by Eric Wolfgang

ISBN: 979-8-9872014-0-4 (paperback)

For my First Reader. She receives my email each day and tells me I'm pretty.

Table of Contents

Argument

My original message read

"React to this,
and I will tell you something true
posted anonymously."

I didn't want to just throw shade at you.

I wanted to throw shade edged
with so much love and regret
that it would confuse you to your grave
if you gave it enough thought.

I wanted you to see the secret side of you
that no fancy arrangement of cameras
or mirrors could capture, no reflections
in the water, no MRIs, no sonic imaging,
no secret sensors or dowsing rods
or precocious little children could show you.

I wanted you to see the parts of your body
that only a lover or a stalker
or a massage therapist could identify
like that birthmark you cover with makeup
to hide your royal ties to a fantasy kingdom.

I wanted to confess my true feelings openly
in anonymous posts, semi-publicly shared,
and read aloud from poetry books.

Because nobody reads poetry books.

Look in this one. I may have written about you.

But I'll never tell.

It Had to Be You

A student caught me off guard with a question.

"Who's your best friend
in the whole building?"

I had to tell them the truth.

I said it was you.

You're welcome.

Slacker

No slacker, you commit
one hundred ten percent to your devotions
unrelated to the work demanded of you.

Because anything demanded of you
can wait.

I've met so many of you
and I accept
that I stand there, too
in good company with the others
who won't do the dishes
who won't sort their email
who won't finish their homework
simply because
someone told you to do it.

And the piles grow around us
ever higher, wild
as the unkept yard
and unironed sheets
scattered as leaves in autumn
and let's face it, every season
because we couldn't be bothered
to pick them up the first time.

Until the undone becomes
too much to live with,
much less see through
because we were so busy working
toward other things.

But think of the Art
you might create,
and think of the Beauty
you will one day stop
to appreciate
even when the house
is on fire, you will pause
to notice

the string of dancing flames
and fail to rescue from the safe
those Important Government Documents.

Let the dishes, let the homework,
let the documents burn,
allow yourself to dance
before the fire.

Remind us why we're friends
and why
I write these poems.

The Strongest Person I Knew

You were the strong one in high school,
the cool girl with the combat boots and skirt
who asked me to hang out with you after school
and I had to say yes.

Don't call it a crush.

Call it an attraction that pulled me
into your field on the day when you needed
someone with you who wasn't your boyfriend.

I couldn't imagine what could terrify
the fierce independent artist you were,
make you ask an idiot sophomore like me
to stand with you, stay close to you.

We waited for everyone to head home
so we could visit the pharmacy unseen,
we ghosted those aisles for minutes
before we lost our nerve, me before you,
even though I couldn't fathom
just what we were afraid of.

We fled to the parking lot
to ride around in shopping carts.
Well, I rode.

You pushed.

I screamed and turned my head to look at you
clomping behind the cart, bandana on your head,
wallet portfolio bouncing against your back,
the strongest person I knew in school
pushing me around to get
better and stronger past fear,
and me in the cart
happy to be there for you.

Warrior's Wig

You're braver than I could ever be
even though we're not traveling
in the same adventure.

I take inspiration from seeing you
wear that dress with
that wig
and moving in them
as if they were assigned
to you at birth.

But to make this less confusing
I must re-state
that I'm not an egg.

I just want to look as happy
with a poem
as you do
in that outfit.

The Audacity

You stood against your teachers
and their simple requests—
take out your pen,
write notes down on paper,
read from a passage,
discuss with your seatmate.

Tall requests for this
compact high school senior.

"The audacity" you called
our expectations as if
us insisting you do something
robbed you of your dignity
and your stature.

I was certain
you didn't know the meaning
of the word audacity,
that you interpreted instruction
as assaults against your personhood
as chains against your freedom.

But you were a Dreamer,
a word that was new to me
even though I grew up
with dreamers
who lived in this country
on the backs of a dream.

So much of our classwork,
so many requests would never
benefit you the way
they benefit this country's
native born citizens—
descendants themselves
of dreamers generations past.

This was the audacity
of your situation.

You live in a country
that promises the world
to its children
except when those children
are born in another country,
then they somehow become
dangerous, suspect,
unwelcome.

The audacity.

You live in a country
where authority figures
don't always have
the best intentions,
so you stand, five feet tall
and bigger
than everyone else in the room
testing "the audacity"
against every "request"
hoping to find strength
to carry through this process
and emerge, fully free.

The audacity.

You are the audacity.

Green Card Stratagem

We hang out in basements and convention halls
and game stores where mostly white gamers
gather to play.

Our melanated skins stand out in stark contrast
to gamers who've done this their entire lives.

Our dreadlocks, our folded eyes,
our curly hair cut short and lined,
our foreign accents—all of it
obvious and pronouncing out loud
that maybe
we don't belong here.

We see and recognize each other for
being who we are, gamers present
to throw dice and chew bubble gum,
but we've long since thrown the dice
and run out of gum or fits to give
about ignorant comments
and sideways assumptions.

We play as hard as anyone else.

You would never assume I was there
to deliver a bag of someone else's takeout
or drive you back to your hotel in a taxi
or that I was lost and looking for the video games.

But it happens.

The disrespect.

People figuring us out and figuring wrong
and figuring that when you're going through your deck
to play a dangerous stratagem
they can ask you, "jokingly,"
if that's your green card
as if you two were always old friends,
as if they knew anything about immigration,
as if they understood that Puerto Rico was a US territory
as if you never needed a green card to begin with.

The disrespect thickens.

They're really asking
if we belong here, or
if someone let us in?

Do we know where these games came from?

Do we know whom these games are for?

But we've arrived, and we claim
these territories on the board
in the name of our countries from across
bodies of water just like their ancestors did,
and we're not moving
and we're not surrendering ground
and we're not delivering their food for them
because we're here for the same reason
as why they're here.

We came to play.

In-Between Games

Before you went to work, you'd wear
your snazzy bartending outfit to game night
in a dingy basement, you were all decked out
in a black vest with white sleeves strapped down
to keep your hands clear to move your pieces.
A wonderful bright red cummerbund
tied the fit together.

You were a vision, moving between
moments of work and play,
between tending bar and teaching,
between dating and marriage,
between youth and fatherhood.

Continue to change
between these moments,
so a little girl can see her dad
in every outfit that you lived in—
as a gamer, as a friend,
as a teacher, as a server,
as everything you were
and everything you want to be,
so she can also clothe herself in
everything she wants to be.

Talk so Much

You talk so much you move
from subject to subject
as if this conversation
is like your last job
hauling freight for companies—
can't stay still for too long before
the work escapes you.

A second later—
you bring up your latest exploits
in roleplaying games as if
a change in topics
was essential as air,
but somewhere
in that endless breath of consciousness
there's always
at least one thing
I never knew before.

One new thing about the world,
or about a company, one new thing about
a movie, a show, or a book.

I force myself to wait, listen patiently,
and learn one new thing about you.

Lost Duels

We traveled miles to compete,
roll dice, measure distances,
share stories of glory and defeat
in battle and in life.

But then, the pandemic.

And then, the quarantine.

Trapped at home, I lost
an edge I had leaned on
so deeply it had sunk beneath
the surface of my skin.

I had lost you and all our friends
and all the social networks in the world
couldn't replace
the sharpness of battle
and the companionship in its aftermath.

In absence I appreciated you
as more than an opponent
so next time we cross the lands
to clash, may the duels be richer
for being fought as friends.

Victory, When it Comes

I count every victory against you,
especially the forfeitures. Without those
I wouldn't have anything except
a love for this game because
when you actually show up to play
you kick my ass from one side
of this four foot table to the other,
handling my game pieces as easily
as if they were your own.

I can't help but notice how wide
the skill gap spans, and how hard
players like me play only to get
devoured by sharks throwing dice.

I have to win some other way,
beyond the bounds of points and scores,
beyond captured territories,
defeated armies and
assassinated generals, but the game's rules
make no conditions
for a diplomatic victory.

Still, I attempt kindness and empathy,
and exchange laughter and stories and
compliments for our painted armies
displayed so dramatically for our
simulated encounter.

We didn't drive 300 miles just to win or lose
some games and then go home—our lives
are larger than that, bigger than the bags we use
to carry our armies from city to city,
wider than our game rating or tournament score.

And still, I can't defeat you. Not in a game,
but I'm in so much good company
that the victories, when they come,
will always be the sweeter for it.

Your company, too.

Your Tournament Judge for Today is Your Mom

"Your mom" is still my favorite tournament judge,
just as she's also still my favorite
gamer tag,
name badge,
avatar handle,
screen name,
punchline,
nemesis,
name scrawled on an application or
filled out in a survey.

She's the best
words said under my breath or
words coughed into my hand or
words said real fast,
however you slice your mom,
her spirit keeps us company
in all gaming walks of life
so tell her I said "Hey" and
I'm sorry I missed your birthday.

Said Just a Word

I never told you that I didn't judge you
for the decisions you had to make when
you were fighting for your survival.

I should have.

I could have said a word, any
to reassure you because
it felt like it was my job to rescue
those who hid from
both words and rescue.

If I had endured
what you endured, what word
could anyone have said
that would have made
life better, or at least
the pain much less awful than
your reaction to a world bent
on twisting your childhood?

I couldn't have said it. Not then.

I can't say it. Even now.

So I never actually told you the word,
and this is me, not actually
saying it because this poem
is addressed anonymously even
as I think of you now because
I'm still too afraid
to say just one word.

Say Her Name

May you never forget
the name of the girl
you were sweating the whole time
you were failing my class.

I should've pulled you off to the side
and into a private conversation
but then what would I say?

"Dude, I got nothing"

Because really, I didn't know
anything about how to deal with
the twin fates
 of failure
and rejection.

But I did know how to pass a class.

"Say her name, then ask her out,
and when she says no return to
the less important task at hand."

"Do this until somebody says yes."

"Eventually someone does."

And then, as if as an afterthought.

"And keep passing classes."

At the Freshman Carnival

As a freshman, you were so slight
I could have gathered you up in my arms
and tossed you out a window.

You were that annoying.

Never mind the "safety precautions" built into
the window stops that only allow someone
to open them for six inches. Freshman you
would have fit.

Somewhere along the way you drank your milk,
exercised, and hulked out while still keeping
that freshman brain that liked so much
to aggravate its teachers.

On the last day of school, years after your graduation,
you loped onto campus swinging arms jacked up
from passing the time lifting heavy weights.

It was the school carnival, and imagine
both our surprises to find me there,
sitting atop the dunk tank, and you,
purchasing three baseballs to accurately hurl
at the trap door trigger.

I never regretted not tossing you out the window
even as I plunged three consecutive times
into the tank full of water.

The Tattoo

When you recommitted to life with a tattoo
inked fresh above the pink scars down your arm,
I realized that I thought I knew you had problems,
but it turns out I didn't know you had problems.

And I kept my questions—the last thing you need
is another inquisitor, but if that's true now, was it true
when you made those cuts?

Could I have stepped in closer to ask you about
the dark space you inhabited, or would that have
driven you even further into it?

And could I have but reached out one arm in a stretch
to enfold you in security, or would that have just
pushed the blade deeper into the wound?

I can only look back at those opportunities lost
and be glad.

We still have you.

Firework Mentor

On the day we taught together,
you watched me quiz the class to see
just how much reading they had done,
and you taught me that
I wasn't doing it for the points,
or for the zeroes,
or for the standards,
or for the literature.

You taught me that I was
figuring out who was lost,
and I've thought about that
for the next decade since.

But then a student moved
on your stapler, and you shut that down,
snapping so fast they were intimidated
by your outsized fury,
and I was caught off guard
that you could burn with such a short fuse.

Other days you turned from
the friendly colleague into fireworks
streaking into the office and exploding
in a display aimed at useless administrations.

You reserved your patience for
a child learning a song,
a student confused by a reading,
a young teacher struggling to fathom
the depths of their own ignorance.

I could have learned so much,
but one day you went off and crackled
off into the sky to bring
your fire and wisdom
to other schools, to other students,
even to other teachers.

You went where you needed to be,
found the places where
you could light up the darkness
and dazzle a watchful audience below.

Someday, I'll figure out where that sky
exists for me.

Outside a Window

He never goes online to update or read his social media,
thinks it's too distant, too impersonal, too cold,
and I never step outside to meet him for lunch or
for dinner,

or to do whatever it is people do beyond their houses,
like it's too close, too personal, too in your face,
but you, his wife, do both, and your posts remind me that
my friend and teacher still exists. He still lives, he still
breathes,

he still enjoys his life with your family tremendously,

and I'm content to exist on the other side of this screen,
looking in, feeling the warmth come through my phone
like the window on a cabin outside in the snow.

Summer Reading

Tortured you with reading to teach you
to love to read, but it turns out it was a stick
that taught you to avoid pain.

I shouldn't have used it.

And you're older now, and I settle for
watching you find inspiration elsewhere
that isn't a book, or a stick, or
an older relative's idea of what's good for you.

I hope it's enough to carry you over
all the obstacles reading was meant
to carry you over.

Failing that, I always have
a list of books I think you'd enjoy.

If you'd still listen to me.

High School Memories

What I confiscated from you in class wasn't
a priceless jewel. Sure, somebody paid for
the cellular device, or the notebook paper you
balled into trash and threw at another student,
or the toy skateboard you used to pretend
you were Tony Hawk with your fingers,
but just think of what I gave you in return—
memories! And they were the best memories,
angry at the teacher kind of memories, talk trash
about an entire school system memories,
reminisce about how the bad days in high school
were so simple kind of memories.

The Worst

The few times I saw you in class
it was impossible to recognize
how far down your problems went.

It took you over a decade to finally
press charges against your father
before you found your courage
to tell the world the truth about why
you were never in class.

The world had taken advantage of you
and then pressed that advantage
throughout your childhood.

I think of some of my worst students,
truant, difficult, struggling to keep up,
some of them might even share
aspects of your story.

And even though you were
never there, you were far
from the worst of students.

The worst student would be a young teacher,
not recognizing trouble sooner.

Intermission

20 reacts and some years later
I can hardly remember whom
each post and poem was dedicated to.

Was it to that friend from high school?

Was it to the gamer from a convention?

Was it to the distant family member living abroad?

Was it to that stranger accidentally friended?

To post anonymously is cowardice,
but to never admit a feeling at all,
to be stoic, to be stone,
to pretend to be immovable as the earth
beneath your feet
even while it's under pressure
from tectonic movement
is far more cowardly.

Still, I make myself
pretend that a poem is not about
the person whom
it's obviously about.

Being brave enough to feel
does not make me brave enough
to confess that feeling
to anyone but myself.

And to you, anonymous reader.

If you find yourself in any of these posts
just imagine
I wrote it for you.

But I'll never tell.

Bubbling Over

When you get so excited about
your latest fandom —
a science fiction show,
a Korean boy band,
a memoir about ramen,
even at this age I can't help but see you
as the five year old who was so happy
to be seen
in their favorite yellow outfit.

"Don't I look so pretty?"

Twirl, twirl, twirl.

Always.

Doppelganger

When they informed us that
the other one existed, our mutuals
were emphatic:

"Oh you should meet
[my name/your name],
the two of you would hit it off."

Not exactly promising.

Well it happened, and we met,
and everything they said
turned out to be true.

I was you, and you were me,
we were warped reflections,
knew each other's jokes so well
that we knew each other.

And I thought—
so THAT's what that's like.

How could I be this annoying?

Internet Friend

Thank you for liking the content that I share,
Internet friend, and posting content for me
to like in return.

Even if I didn't know you before, it feels like
we've grown to know each other now, even after
accidentally friending each other
through a mutual acquaintance.

This feels like it could be one of those hidden
positive feedback loops that feed into the universe,
driving the great machine forward,
and making it possible to truly live.

IRL Friends

We argued whether my Internet friends
could ever count as my "real friends"
because you always sought to connect with people
"IRL" (as Internet friends like to say),

Even with me. A nerd connected
through keyboard and screen in an age
before the ubiquity of cellphones
and social networks.

But who was there when I announced
my marriage proposal?

The Dragon Raid.

And who was there when I ranted about work
while listening to others rant about work?

The Group Chat.

And who was there when I learned to paint,
taught me new techniques and geeked out
about new things to paint?

The Message Forums.

And who was there when I posted both
the death of my father and the upcoming
birth of my son on the same day?

The Friends List.

We no longer work together.

You moved, like so many IRL friends passing
through Chicago. Moved on to better things
in different places, leaving me behind here
to try to make new friends.

But if I messaged you, commented on your posts,
liked and subscribed to your videos and pictures,
would you feel that warmth I still have for you
even though you're not here in my life today?

Because I would message you, I would
comment on your posts, I would still
like and subscribe and feel the warmth
because you haven't really left me.
None of you have.

Friends Passing Through Chicago

This is not a eulogy.

I often wish that we could have been
closer friends than we were during
the years you lived in Chicago.

You haven't died, but the distance
has only grown louder as you become
the amalgamation of my friends
passing through this city.

Teaching, gaming, falling in love,
I wrote this for all of you hoping
that sharing a regret does not multiply it,
I divide regret like my attention
which can only go so far.

Follow so many stories on my feed
before I lose track of you again,
one after the other, until it becomes
as if you never lived here,
as if we never met,
as if we were never friends.

Here. In Chicago.

Oldest Internet Friend

And how is my oldest Internet friend?
We've survived college, adulthood, careers,
orphanage, fatherhood. We've never lived
within the same time zone or state boundaries,
and every milestone has been different—
success, failure, despair, happiness.

And yet you've always understood me
across these electronic worlds.

I've always looked forward to seeing you
when circumstances allowed us to cross
these borders between our lives. Like ghosts
we see each other for an instant before
the world demands corporeality.

In that same world changing around us,
I've focused on you when I was lost
and needed to find a path back to myself.

We crossed these differences as easily
as we might cross a room, so comfortable
it felt to be together.

So where to next? What lies beyond?
Our lives continue on their separate orbits
around this rock. Minute decays over time
could mean we might not meet again
until death.

Maybe we can pick up this friendship after that?

I'd like that.

Polycomradery

I know we both like to annoy each other
and I know we've both been married
to other people for decades at this point,
but I just think
if we each happened to become single
maybe we could come to an agreement
to spend the next decades of our lives
annoying each other still
as two single people.

Fat Bodies in Cheap Hotels

When I try to sleep on a poorly made mattress,
I remember what you once told me about fat bodies
trying to settle in cheap hotel beds.

You said they never do.

And now I can't sleep on a rollout, on a couch bed,
on a foam mattress in a college dormitory. I'm too busy
paying attention to how my poorly maintained body
fails to distribute its own weight in a way
that makes sleep possible.

The fat is always in the way.

I suppose I could run, I suppose I could eat better,
I suppose I could just spend the money and find
a nicer bed in a more expensive hotel
that would solve this problem for just a few nights.

But hotel stays end, I carry my fat home
to a bed I've long since learned how to sleep in
and I can make better decisions after I wake up.

Or I can just make the same ones.

Tides of Fat

Follow you online, follow in your footsteps,
and follow your waistline
that shifts back and forth like the tide.

It moves as if the Moon's own gravity
summons it from its place and sends it
back again. This whole time your footprints
in the sand have remained the same size
despite the insistent calls of gravity,
of age, of dark matter that pulls
upon our heavenly bodies.

As I write this I watch you
fight the tides and transform yourself
into a young man again, the kind
who publicly buys himself new clothing
to fit into an old shape you've returned to.

I need you to know that you inspire me
as much as you terrify me. I don't know
if I can walk, or run, in those footsteps again.

Too Loud

Weeks after you started,
our colleague asked me
if you were as mean as you spoke,
but you never were.

You were intense and said
what was on your mind in a voice
stronger and louder
than people expected you to use.

You weren't just loud,
you were confident,
you weren't just bold,
you were the newest teacher
in the building.

You asked questions
that were on our minds
but we didn't dare ask.

You were bigger than that.

You were bigger, your voice was louder,
and even your work with students
spoke for itself.

If that makes you mean, then
I should have said yes.

You're the meanest.

Homeroom Delinquent

I was a new teacher and
you were never officially on my roster.

What could I have said to a senior
determined to leave his class
and sit cross-legged on the gym floor
beside my homeroom every day?

You read anything except the books
assigned to you by your teachers
that you needed to make it
to graduation in June.

You made it anyway,
as a member of the audience,
there to celebrate your friends
in my homeroom, and photobomb
our group shot, your dark outfit
standing out against our robes.

I still have that picture of us.

Sometimes I think I could have
given you different books to read
because too many of us believe
that a book recommendation
can rescue a lost soul.

Because it's worked for so many of us.

And sometimes I think,
we should've talked more,
but maybe that's why you broke free
from your homeroom teacher—
too much talk, none of it helpful.

Maybe the best would've been
to let you sit with us, let you
do what you needed.

Let time run its course.

Let graduation pass.

Let you find your own books.

Recommend a few titles.

If you asked.

Still Haven't Found

Never asked you to find those tickets for me
to see U2 perform at Soldier Field among
the memorials to fallen veterans, I'd only be out
a few hundred dollars and my voice
blasted from singing along to more songs
from their catalog than I'd care to admit,
but it still would have been a wild time,
a more innocent time, unlike today
with thousands dead at the hands of plague
and Bono performing underground
beneath a literal warzone for veterans
actively fighting to defend their country.

And I thought I was afraid of crowds back then.

Now, that concert is just another hole in my life
that regret tries to fill, but there's not enough dirt
to finish the job properly, and I still have my life,
and I still have my freedom, and I still have
this friendship that has survived
across the years and borders where we've lived
separately when you offered to help me
and I never thanked you for that.

Two Teachers

Our teaching experiences have been
so different between our two states—
I wonder how anyone could leave
the classroom behind, just as you wonder
how anyone would want to stay.

You were probably the better teacher.

It's obvious in the way you interact
with family, with friends, with strangers,
and with me.

And every day people like you leave
where the pay and conditions are untenable,
and every day people like me soldier on
wondering if the pay is enough to make
the conditions more bearable.

You wonder if there's a career out there
to support you and your dreams,
and I wonder if there's a career in here
that can support the same in me.

The Pursuit of Something Else

Watching you leave our career,
the safety of a steady paycheck, benefits,
and me to follow the uncertainty of open seas
in dogged pursuit of your passion
made me wonder—could I ever be so moved
to leave where I've sat for over 20 years now
to pursue the outer limits of my own desires,
to forgo food, mortgage, healthcare,
and the luxuries a stable paycheck provided
to work instead at scratching words
into unstructured verse
and just make a living doing anything else
aside from teaching.

Just like that.

Or do this on the side, and in secret
like I'm ashamed of poetry,
and each day that you're gone reminds me
that I, too, could just let go of the securities
of employment and classroom,
reach for the flying handles
of this poetry
that I love so much.

Just like that.

Be here for years, then disappear
from everyone's lives
to write something in this world
like this poem, but then
just what would I have to say?

Intermission, Closer to the End

These poems make me into a giant Magic 8 Ball,
far less accurate, and far less specific than
a pyramid floating in mysterious black ink.

You have to shake me harder than that
to reveal my answers in the light,
or on paper,
or inside of a digital document.

The answer surfaces
from deep inside my pitch black darkness,
a truth etched onto a floating tetrahedron
waiting for Archimedes' Law
to release it in a post,
or unleash it
in a poem.

Ready to be read
and rejected.

Less ready
to be accepted or ignored.

One Year to Become Friends

You were my favorite person in all of high school,
but maybe high school was the worst time
to spend so little of it with our favorites.

We saw each other for a year before you left,
when you brightened the hallways
and lunch periods when you were truant.

We kept in touch, but you left again,
and then again,
constantly moving on a trajectory
further away towards your own destiny
nowhere near a high school
or its memory.

I didn't leave, but remaining
has its own trajectory, its own destination,
its own destiny,
I spun my own life out
in directions
further from you.

Until gravity and adulthood
found us in this city again
with our own families
with our own careers
maybe high school would have been
brighter to have you there longer
but I love us like this.

Two travelers accumulating lives
separate from each other
and sharing light whenever
we come near.

There and Back Again

Each year you've knocked
on the rounded door of my isolated hobbit hole
where I've always been content
to tend to my own fields and not bother with
an outside world that wasn't bothering me,
but you knocked and came with
your wagon and your friends
and your invitation to sing and share
a month of writing poetry.

And so I blame you for these adventures
into the deep dark woods. Every year I emerge
from the forest and blink my eyes
at the strange company we've kept
through cavernous kingdoms
where a dragon always waits,
and the deeper tunnels
where a riddle always hides.

We've gone, there and back again,
returned with the only treasures we claimed—
songs we've always known but whose tunes and lyrics
we had to discover.

And though the roads ahead may go ever
ever on, thank you for bringing me along on this one.

Apex Extroverts

Not all of my extrovert friends are predatory,
stalking conversation and attention
like it's a meal that can sate their appetites,
but you've been feasting for so long
on us awkward gaming introverts
that you might have lost a step
out in the wild.

Other apex extroverts sense
your softness to dorkwads,
your empathy, your kindness, your calm.

Face it, a diet of us has infected you,
to protect us from harm, from other predators,
from ourselves,
and in exchange we've learned
a bit of your fierceness,
a bit of your pride.

You are always so much, but
you never allow yourself
to become too much for quiet nerds everywhere
reliant on your ministrations,
even when our natural tendencies
keep us from saying so out loud.

You know. You understand.

You continue on a path that's
inextricably linked with ours.

It's enough most times
to keep the wolves away
and keep us warm and safe.

For the Poem You Sent in 2020

I'm sorry.

I couldn't say then how much
I enjoyed your poem.

There was a pandemic
followed by riots
and all this time
there have been
extrajudicial killings
in the background to my experience.

They escaped my conscience.

I wasn't aware how
frequently life challenges
the people I love.

And the poetry that they write.

It was beautiful.

So Many Goodbyes

When we went to the hospital
to visit our sick friend, we were still
so innocent about hospital illnesses.

We even brought a card.

I told the two of you to behave
before we got there, so you linked hands
and skipped along like children.

We were all idiots that day, working off
of nervous energy.

They had him laid out in his room,
surrounded by his family whose heads
were low and their voices lower.

They accepted our card with a quiet thanks
before returning to each other with their
whispers, offering nothing to us
except for quiet condemnation.

The final proof—
blood slipped from his mouth, blood that
a brother, cousin, uncle, or friend
gently wiped from his face
and waited for us to leave.

It was a long series of goodbyes,
from the day he went to see his doctor
to the funeral, to the time we spent together
honoring his memory.

I said goodbye to you soon after as well,
time and circumstance drawing us apart
with our missing friend a constant reminder
how little time we have left.

When I see you, I sometimes wonder
what will be the trickle of blood to signal
that it's time for one of us to go
and speak our final goodbyes?

I hope it never happens.

You can live on inside my memories
without pain, or auguries of death,
without blood on your lips
or family surrounding your body,
you can go on and live forever.

Back Home

I could have been at your wedding
far across the sea. I could have afforded
the flight and time off work, but not even
my love for you could overcome
my irrational fear for the islands
my parents referred to as "Back Home."

It's a fear as irrational as fear of Chicago—
the violence doesn't affect you
until the day that it does, and the bullets
have less likelihood of striking you
than I have of buying tickets
to visit "Back Home."

I didn't go with my dad when he visited
Back Home for the very last time, so I was
a globe away when he fell in the shower
and died too far from where
medical attention could have reached him.

And I didn't visit my brother when he moved
Back Home for years. There he had a child
who would be the same age as my son.
We didn't meet him until they flew out themselves.

Because I wouldn't go there.

But for you two, I should have
overcome my fears, bought the tickets,
renewed my passport,
brought my family along.

Maybe I could have proven to myself
that back home wasn't so frightening,
that I could be closer to my loved ones,
that we could be closer, even now.

Maybe I could have connected
with my family's story, deepened my roots
in Back Home's thick jungles,
breathed in the heavy traffic
of Back Home's capital city,
danced in the light of the bonfires
set ablaze on dried coconut husks.

Maybe I could have done enough,
so I wouldn't have had to write this poem.

On Fathers Dying in Another Country

You were always with him.

Never mind the pandemic, the long journey,
the mandatory quarantine, the years past
since you last met, the long years to come
where so many of us live without our fathers.

It was only his body that gave up, that laid itself
to rest, that told him that it was time to go.

Had you crossed the barriers sooner,
he might have, too, relieved at your impending arrival,
comforted by the thought that his child
was attempting to come home.

It's all we fathers want, for our children
to return, in body or in mind, even just
in their hearts would be enough. To remember
that we live on as memory, as part of their skin,
as an acquired habit or tic,
as a thinly held interest.

Our children will travel any distance
when they're ready, and some part of us
will be waiting for them before we go
to welcome them home.

A Turn in the Woods

Got lost for a bit
in anxiety that made me
lose my footing on the trail,
but
you were there, and
you were calm, and
you spoke a kind word
which is when I realized
that I needed it all to find
my position back on the map
and walk my way home.

Love Letter

I apologize for all the illegible love letters.

Words, when they come, come out wrong
and misshapen by my intentions.

I have to clarify with my hands
what gets lost in my penmanship
and trace into your skin
the patterns you desire.

Who I Write For

"Who are you writing for?"

Your question, when it finally lands
stuns me into a daylong silence.
I still live my life, travel to and from work,
interact with students, colleagues, family,
the coffee baristas, the necessary email,
I even make a few jokes on my feed,
but the question processes subliminally
like a trauma. I even pause at my work
on this book to ponder
each time the question rises
into my surface thoughts
as doubt, as cancer, as pain.

But the answer, when it comes,
has always been evident.

I write for myself, the rest of you
are collateral damage.

For friends, for family, for students,
for strangers I met on the Internet,
each one a part of me just like
you are a part of me. I sit in my desk
and write about us like it's my job
and because I'm under this delusion
that my confessions could mean
something to anybody but me.
So, stay a minute. Listen to me sing.

Even if it's not written for you,
it can be about you.

Final Post

I wish I could find the words
that would make you hear me
then you could be
my only reader.

Acknowledgements

First of all, thank you to everyone who reacted to my original post on social media. You drove me to write specific memories for each of you that somehow started to seem like they applied to other people in my life as well. No shade was actually thrown in the making of this book. Just sincere love and admiration. If you felt any of that then I've succeeded in some small part.

I'd also like to thank former student and current cover artist, Eric Wolfgang. He talked me through some of this publishing stuff and also made me look cooler than I ever was IRL. I think the cover is cooler than the poems, even.

And thanks to Laura Bolesta for editing the book and giving me a usable template for publishing. She repaired some of the odd formatting I had in the original document. Although she claims she doesn't want credit because it attracts more work, she's fully deserving of both the credit and the right to not do more work.

Special thanks go out to Iris Orpi and Will Reger for nudging me in the right direction artistically. I can't match them for talent, but it won't hurt me to try.

As hinted before, my wife Tara "gets" to read everything that I write each day, and to our son who forces me to use my computer when he's not on it playing games. They both inspire me and make me more productive.

As for the solution to who each poem was about—I'll never tell, but some of them already know. Thank you.

www.ingramcontent.com/pod-product-compliance
Lightning Source LLC
LaVergne TN
LVHW051607080426
835510LV00020B/3175